Wheat-Free Classics

Dessert and Baking Recipes

Dessert Recipes

Introduction

Imagine enjoying a rich, delicious dessert and afterward feeling great about it. That is the goal of this recipe book. You will find a collection of dessert recipes that are created without any flour or grains. Other ingredients that are surely not found here are refined sugars or processed foods. Nature has provided just what is needed for a delicious and nutritious dessert without any of the artificial flavors or harmful processing. Discover how to use fruits, raw honey, agave nectar, raw chocolate and more to create desserts that hit the spot!

The main hurdle in losing unwanted weight is sticking to a healthy diet. When a craving strikes, sometimes that ice cream cone or chocolate chip cookie may be irresistible. Fear not, dessert lovers! We are programmed to run on sugar and nature has provided everything we need. Keep these recipes, and maybe even an emergency batch of healthy cookies, on hand at all times to get nutrients your body needs along with a satisfying treat. When you taste how delicious these desserts are, you won't believe they are actually good for you too. Stick to your weight loss goals and feel great while experimenting with these all natural desserts!

Table of Contents

Banana Bread Pudding
Simply Sweet Potato Blondie
Coconut Cream Pie
Pecan Chess Pies
Wild Mince Meat Pie
Almond Butter Balls
Baked Peaches
Perfect Refrigerator Fudge
Dessert Pizza
Tiramisu
Mixed Berry Trifle
Sugar Cookies
Carrot Cake Cookies
Chocolate Almond Biscotti
Chocolate Mousse
Vanilla Pudding
Frozen Chocolate Cherry Custard
Ginger Mango Sherbet
Sweet Potato Gnocchi
Flourless Chocolate Cake
Apple Dump Muffins
Pumpkin Spice Cakes
Fruit And Nut Cake

Toasted Almond Cream Cakes
Pineapple Upside Down Cake

Banana Bread Pudding

Prep Time: 10 minutes

Cook Time: 30 minutes

Servings: 12

INGREDIENTS

Banana Bread

1 cup of almond flour

2 eggs

2 overripe bananas

1/4 cup sweetener*

2 tablespoons coconut oil

1 tablespoon baking powder

1 tablespoon cinnamon

1 teaspoon nutmeg

1 teaspoon vanilla

1/2 teaspoon of sea salt

Banana Custard

13 oz (1 can) full-fat coconut milk

6 egg yolks

1 overripe banana

1/4 cup sweetener*

1/4 cup raisins

1/2 cup dried pitted dates

2 tablespoons tapioca starch/flour

2 teaspoons vanilla

1 teaspoon cinnamon

Pinch sea salt

INSTRUCTIONS

1. Preheat oven to 350 degrees F. Line muffin pan with paper liners or coat with coconut oil.
2. In medium mixing bowl, beat 2 eggs, 2 bananas, 2 tablespoons oil and 1/4 cup sweetener with hand mixer or whisk.
3. In separate mixing bowl, add 1 cup almond flour, 1 tablespoon baking powder, 1 tablespoon cinnamon, 1 teaspoon nutmeg, 1 teaspoon vanilla and 1/2 teaspoon salt.
4. Pour banana mixture into flour mixture and mix well.
5. Pour batter into muffin pan and bake for about 15 minutes, or until golden brown, risen and firm.
6. While muffins cook, add coconut milk, egg yolks, banana, sweetener, vanilla, cinnamon and salt to medium bowl and blend briefly with hand mixer or whisk.
7. Pour into medium pot and heat over medium heat. Chop dates and add to pot with raisins.
8. Stir in tapioca flour. Stir as *Banana Custard* thickens, about 5 minutes. Remove from heat.
9. Remove muffins from oven and turn out onto cutting board.
10. Increase oven to 375 degrees F. Lightly coat square or rectangular baking dish with coconut oil.
11. Carefully remove paper liners and roughly chop muffins. Add muffin chunks to baking dish. Pour banana custard over chopped muffins.
12. Place dish in oven and bake for 15 minutes.

13. Remove and allow to cool for 15 minutes before serving.

14. Serve warm or room temperature.

stevia, raw honey or agave nectar

Simply Sweet Potato Blondie

Prep Time: 15 minutes

Cook Time: 30 minutes

Servings: 12

INGREDIENTS

2/3 cups coconut flour

2 tablespoons arrowroot powder

1 large sweet potato

4 eggs

3/4 cup sweetener*

1/4 cup full-fat coconut milk

1/4 cup cacao butter

1/2 teaspoon baking powder

2 tablespoons vanilla

Pinch sea salt

Pinch ground white pepper (or black pepper)

INSTRUCTIONS

1. Preheat oven to 350 degrees F. Grease an 9 x 13 inch pan or "all-corner" specialty brownie pan with coconut oil. Bring medium pot of lightly salted water to boil.
2. Peel and dice sweet potato. Add to boiling water for 5 - 10 minutes, until soft.
3. Beat eggs in medium mixing bowl with hand mixer or whisk. Add sweetener, coconut milk, vanilla and pepper until combined.

4. Sift in flour, arrowroot powder, baking powder and salt, and mix until combined.

5. Drain sweet potatoes and add to small mixing bowl with cacao butter. Beat or mash until cacao butter is well melted. Add sweet potato mixture to egg mixture.

6. Scrape batter into baking pan and smooth top with spatula.

7. Bake for 25 - 30 minutes, until center is firm and top is golden brown. Toothpick inserted into center will come out moist but mostly clean.

8. Allow to cool about 10 minutes. Slice and serve warm or room temperature.

*stevia, raw honey or agave nectar

Coconut Cream Pie

Prep Time: 20 minutes*

Cook Time: 20 minutes

Servings: 8

INGREDIENTS

Crust

1/2 cup soft nuts**

1 cup almond flour

2 teaspoons sweetener***

1/4 - 1/2 cup coconut oil

Filling

26 oz (2 cans) full-fat coconut milk

2 eggs

1/2 cup arrowroot powder

1/4 cup sweetener*

1 tablespoon vanilla

1 cup flaked coconut

Pinch sea salt

INSTRUCTIONS

1. Preheat oven to 350 degrees F. Lightly coast pie plate with coconut oil.
2. Grind nuts into coarse meal with food processor or bullet blender. Add to small bowl with almond flour, 2 tablespoons sweetener and enough coconut oil to bring together soft but crumbly dough.

3. Press dough into pie plate and bake about 10 - 15 minutes, until crust becomes golden.

4. Remove crust from oven and allow to cool. Turn off oven.

5. Add coconut milk, eggs, arrowroot powder, sweetener, vanilla and salt to medium pot. Heat pot over medium heat and bring to a boil. Stir constantly as mixture thickens.

6. Stir in 1/2 cup shredded coconut. Then pour the filling over the crust.

7. *Refrigerate pie until filling is set, about 4 hours.

8. Heat medium pan over medium heat. Add 1/2 cup flaked coconut and toast about 5 minutes. Stir frequently to prevent burning.

9. Sprinkle toasted coconut over pie and serve chilled.

NOTE: Line springform pan with parchment and bake crust, then fill with coconut cream filling for another version of **Coconut Cream Pie**.

*coconut flakes, pecans, walnuts, cashews or brazil nuts
***stevia, raw honey or agave nectar

Pecan Chess Pies

Prep Time: 20 minutes

Cook Time: 25 minutes

Servings: 6

INGREDIENTS

Crust

1 1/2 cups almond flour

1/2 cup pecans

1 egg

2 tablespoons coconut oil

1/4 teaspoon sea salt

Filling

1 cup full-fat coconut milk

2 cups pecans

1 cup dried pitted dates

1/2 cup sweetener*

2 eggs

2 egg yolks

1 1/2 tablespoons arrowroot powder

2 tablespoons coconut oil

1 teaspoon vanilla

INSTRUCTIONS

1. Preheat oven to 350 degrees F. Coat 6 mini pie plates or pie pans with coconut oil. Bring small pot of water to boil, leaving room for dates.

2. Add dates to boiling water for about 5 - 10 minutes, until tender. Then drain.

3. For *Crust*, process pecans in food processor or bullet lender until well ground. Add to small mixing bowl with almond flour and salt. Mix in oil and egg until dough forms.

4. Press dough into pie plates with hand or wooden spoon. Bake about 10 minutes, until golden. Remove pie shells from oven and set aside.

5. Chop 1 cup pecans and set aside

6. For *Filling*, process softened dates in food processor or bullet blender with about half of coconut milk. Add to medium mixing bowl with remaining coconut milk, sweetener, eggs, egg yolks, coconut oil, vanilla and arrowroot powder. Beat with hand mixer or whisk until combined and a bit airy. Mix in chopped pecans.

7. Pour batter into mini pie crusts. Top with whole pecans and bake for 20 - 25 minutes, until filling is set.

8. Remove pies and let cool about 20 minutes before serving.

9. Serve warm. Or refrigerate and serve cold. Also great at room temperature.

*stevia, raw honey or agave nectar

NOTE: For large **Pecan Chess Pie**, bake in 9-inch pie plate for 45 - 55 minutes, or until center is set.

Wild Mince Meat Pie

Prep Time: 20 minutes

Cook Time: 30 minutes

Servings: 8

INGREDIENTS

Crust

4 cups almond flour

2 eggs

1/4 cup coconut oil

1/2 teaspoon sea salt

Filling

12 oz grass-fed beef

2 sweet apples

2 tart apples

1 cup beef stock

1/4 cup sweetener*

Juice of 1 orange

Zest of 1 orange

1/4 cup arrowroot powder

1/4 cup apple cider vinegar

1 cup raisins

1/2 cup dried pitted dates

1/2 cup dried pitted prunes

1/2 cup dried cherries

2 teaspoons ground cinnamon

1 teaspoon ground nutmeg

1/2 teaspoon ground cloves

1/2 teaspoon ground black pepper

1/2 teaspoon salt

INSTRUCTIONS

1. Preheat oven to 350 degrees F. Heat large pot over medium-high heat and lightly coat with coconut oil. Lightly oil pie plate. Prepare 4 sheets of parchment.

2. Place beef in hot oiled pan and brown on each side for about 5 - 7 minutes, until just cooked through. Remove beef and set aside. Add beef stock to pot.

3. Mix all *Crust* ingredients together in medium bowl until dough forms. Divide dough in half and use rolling pin to roll dough between two parchment sheets into circles to fit about 1 inch over pie plate.

4. Press one dough circle into pie plate. Crimp edges to create small lip. Bake for 5 minutes, then remove and set aside.

5. Peel, core and grate or dice apples. Add to beef stock with sweetener, zest and juice of orange, vinegar, raisins, cherries, spices and salt. Dice beef, prunes and dates, and add to pot. Stir in arrowroot powder and thicken for a few minutes.

6. Once mixture comes together pour into par baked pie shell. Top with second dough sheet and crimp edges to fit into bottom crust.

7. Use sharp knife to slice top crust a few times for venting.

8. Bake pie for 30 minutes, or until crust is golden brown.

9. Remove from oven and allow to cool for about 20 minutes.

10. Slice and serve warm. Or allow to cool completely and serve room temperature.

stevia, raw honey or agave nectar

Almond Butter Balls

Prep Time: 10 minutes

Cook Time: 10 minutes

Servings: 12

INGREDIENTS

1/2 cup almond butter

1/2 cup almonds

1/4 cup cashews

1 tablespoon cocoa powder

1 tablespoon ground chia seed (or flax meal)

5 dried pitted dates

3/4 cup flaked coconut

2 tablespoons sweetener*

1 teaspoon cinnamon

INSTRUCTIONS

1. Heat small pot over high heat. Add cashews and enough water to cover. Boil cashews until softened, about 8 minutes.
2. Add softened cashews to food processor or bullet blender with sweetener, and process until smooth. Add water to thin if mixture is too thick or chunky. Scrape into small mixing bowl.
3. Chop dates and almonds by hand or in food processor or bullet blender. Add to cashew cream with almond butter and mix together.
4. Add cocoa powder, chia or flax meal, coconut and cinnamon, and blend.

5. Add 1 tablespoon at a time of almond butter or cocoa powder to get mixture to perfect consistency to hold together as a ball.
6. Use mini scoop or tablespoon to portion twelve servings. Roll each serving into a ball. Place balls on parchment covered half sheet pan or plate and refrigerate for about 20 minutes.
7. Serve chilled or room temperature.

stevia, raw honey or agave nectar

Baked Peaches

Prep Time: 5 minutes

Cook Time: 25 minutes

Servings: 4

INGREDIENTS

2 ripe peaches

1/4 cup walnuts

1/4 cup dried cranberries

2 tablespoons sweetener*

Juice of 1 orange

Zest of 1 orange

1 teaspoon cinnamon

1/2 teaspoon nutmeg

1/2 teaspoon ground allspice

INSTRUCTIONS

1. Preheat oven to 375 degrees F.
2. Slice peaches in half and remove pit. Place peach halves into glass or ceramic baking dish just big enough for them to fit snuggly.
3. Chop walnuts and toss with cranberries, sweetener, spices, juice and zest of orange in small bowl.
4. Fill peach halves with fruit and nut mixture. Pour excess liquid over peaches.
5. Bake in oven for about 20 - 25 minutes, until peaches are soften and lightly browned.
6. Remove from oven and let cool about 5 minutes.

7. Serve warm or room temperature.

stevia, raw honey or agave nectar

Perfect Refrigerator Fudge

Prep Time: 10* minutes

Cook Time: 5 minutes

Servings: 6

INGREDIENTS

1/4 cup cocoa powder

1/2 cup almond butter (or 3/4 cup almonds)

1/2 cup hazelnut butter (or 1/2 cup hazelnuts)

2 tablespoons coconut oil

1/4 cup sweetener*

1/4 cup walnuts

1/4 cup chopped

INSTRUCTIONS

1. Line square baking dish with parchment paper.
2. To make nut butter, process 3/4 cup almonds and 1/2 cup hazelnuts in food processor or bullet blender. Blend until fairly smooth. Add coconut oil to thin if necessary.
3. Chop remaining walnuts and hazelnuts. Add to small bowl with nut butters, cocoa powder, remaining coconut oil and sweetener and mix well.
4. *Spread mixture into parchment lined baking dish and refrigerate for about 2 - 3 hours.
5. Slice and serve chilled or room temperature.

* raw honey, agave nectar or maple syrup

Dessert Pizza

Prep Time: 15 minutes*

Cook Time: 20 minutes

Servings: 8

INGREDIENTS

Crust

1 medium sweet potato

1 cup almond flour

2 eggs

1/4 cup tapioca flour

1 1/2 teaspoon baking powder

1 teaspoon ground cinnamon

1 teaspoon sea salt

Topping

13 oz (1 can) full-fat coconut milk

2 egg yolks

1 tablespoon tapioca powder

Juice of lemon half

Zest if lemon half

1 teaspoon vanilla

4 dried figs

1/4 cup dried apricots

1/4 cup dried cranberries

1/3 cup dried cherries

INSTRUCTIONS

1. Preheat oven to 350 degrees F. Bring medium pot of lightly salted water to a boil. Cover sheet pan with parchment paper, baking mat, or aluminum foil coated with coconut oil.

2. Peel and dice sweet potato. Add sweet potato and figs to pot and boil 5 - 10 minutes, or until soft.

3. While potatoes boil, heat small pot over medium heat. Add coconut milk, egg yolks, 1 tablespoon tapioca flour, juice and zest of half a lemon. Stir until thickened, about 5 - 10 minutes. Remove from heat and set aside.

4. Drain sweet potatoes and figs in colander. Set figs aside to cool. Add sweet potatoes to medium mixing bowl and mash with hand mixer or whisk. Add 2 eggs and beat well. Then mix in, almond flour, tapioca flour, baking powder, cinnamon and salt with wooden spoon to form dough.

5. Place dough on sheet pan and cover with parchment sheet. Press into round disc with palms, then flatten with rolling pin if desired. Remove top parchment sheet.

6. Bake crust for 20 minutes until center is firm and edges are lightly browned.

7. Chop softened figs and apricots.

8. Carefully remove crust and turn oven to broil. Evenly spread coconut lemon sauce over crust and sprinkle with dried fruit.

9. Return pizza to oven and broil for 2 minutes, just to heat toppings.

10. Remove pizza from oven. Slice and serve warm.

* stevia, raw honey or agave nectar*

Tiramisu

Prep Time: 20 minutes*

Cook Time: 10 minutes

Servings: 8

INGREDIENTS

Lady Fingers

1/3 cup coconut flour

3 tablespoons arrowroot powder

4 eggs

1/4 cup sweetener**

1/2 teaspoon baking powder

1/2 teaspoon vanilla

2 tablespoons instant espresso (or instant coffee)

3/4 cup water

2 tablespoons cocoa powder

Cashew Mascarpone

2 cups cashews

2 tablespoons sweetener**

1 teaspoon lemon juice

1 teaspoon vanilla

Water

INSTRUCTIONS

1. *Soak 2 cups cashews in water overnight. Drain and rinse.

2. Preheat oven to 400 degrees F. Line two sheet pans with parchment paper. Fit pastry bag with 1/2 inch round tube, or cut 1/4 inch corner off sturdy kitchen storage bag (like Ziploc®).

3. Beat egg yolks, 1/4 cup sweetener and 1/2 teaspoon vanilla until thick and pale.

4. In separate bowl beat egg whites to stiff peaks with hand mixer or whisk in medium bowl. Fold half of egg whites into egg yolk mixture. Then sift in coconut flour, arrowroot powder and baking powder. Fold in remaining egg whites.

5. Scoop batter into pastry bag or storage bag. Place in tall wide contain and fold open end of bag over edge of container for greater ease.

6. Pipe 5 inch lady fingers onto parchment lined sheet pans about 2 inches apart. Bake for 8 minutes.

7. Remove cookies from oven and transfer full parchment sheet onto wire rack to cool completely. Do not try to remove warm cookies from parchment.

8. Process soaked cashews in food processor or bullet blender with sweetener, lemon juice, vanilla, and just enough water to smooth.

9. Bring 3/4 cup water just under a boil. Dissolve instant espresso or coffee in water and add to shallow dish.

10. Remove cooled lady fingers form parchment. Dip and roll each cookie in espresso, then arrange in single layer in glass baking dish. Cut cookies to fit into tight layer.

11. Dollop and spread on half of *Cashew Mascarpone*. Then add another layer of espresso dipped lady fingers. Top with last half of *Cashew Mascarpone* and sift on cocoa powder.

12. *Refrigerate at least 30 - 60 minutes.

13. Slice and serve chilled.

*stevia, raw honey or agave nectar

Mixed Berry Trifle

Prep Time: 10 minutes

Cook Time: 25 minutes

Servings: 12

INGREDIENTS

Cake

1 cup almond flour

1 cup coconut flour

3/4 cup coconut milk

4 eggs

1/2 cup sweetener*

1/2 cup coconut oil

2 tablespoons vanilla

2 teaspoons baking soda

Filling

1 cup coconut cream

2 tablespoons sweetener*

1 cup strawberries

1/2 cup blueberries

1/2 cup raspberries

1/2 cup blackberries

Juice of orange half

Juice of lemon half

Zest of orange half

Zest of lemon half

1/4 cup pistachios

INSTRUCTIONS

1. Preheat oven to 350 degrees F. Line muffin pan with paper liner or coat with coconut oil.
2. In large mixing bowl, beat eggs and coconut milk until light and airy. Beat in sweetener, oil and vanilla.
3. Sift in almond flour, coconut flour and baking soda. Mix until well combined.
4. Use ice cream scoop or spoon to scoop batter into muffin pan. Fill each cup 1/2 - 2/3 full with batter.
5. Bake in for about 15 minutes, until firm but springy in the center.
6. Remove cupcakes from oven and turn out onto wire rack or plate. Allow to cool for about 10 minutes and remove paper liners.
7. Dice strawberries and add to medium bowl with blueberries, raspberries, blackberries, lemon and orange zests and juices. Toss to combine.
8. In small bowl, mixi coconut cream with 2 tablespoon sweetener.
9. Slice cupcake in half to create top and bottom. Dollop coconut cream onto bottom half, then top with a spoonful of fruit. Drain juice from spoon before adding to cake.
10. Place cupcake top on top of fruit. Press down slightly. Add another dollop of coconut cream and another spoonful of fruit. Repeat with remaining cupcakes.
11. Serve room temperature. Or chill for 30 minutes and serve.

NOTE: Bake cake in 3 round cake pans for 20 minutes, then layer with cream and berries and stack for **Mixed Berry Trifle Cake**.

*stevia, raw honey or agave nectar

Sugar Cookies

Prep Time: 10 minutes

Cook Time: 15 minutes

Servings: 12

INGREDIENTS

1 1/2 cups almond flour

1 cup coconut flour

1/2 cup sweetener*

5 dried pitted dates

1 egg

2 teaspoons coconut oil

1 teaspoon vanilla

1/2 teaspoon baking soda

Pinch sea salt

Water

INSTRUCTIONS

1. Preheat oven to 350 degrees F. Line sheet pan with parchment paper. Bring small pot of water to boil. Add dates and boil for about 5 - 8 minutes, until softened.

2. Add dates to food processor or bullet blender and process until smooth. Add leftover water if necessary.

3. Add sweetener, egg, oil and vanilla to dates and process until smooth.

4. Add date mixture to medium bowl. Sift in almond flour, coconut flour baking soda and salt. Beat with hand mixer until combined and smooth, about 5 minutes.

5. Roll dough into a log about 3 inches in diameter. Slice into 1/4 inch thick disks.

6. Place disks on sheet pan and bake for about 8 - 10 minutes.

7. Remove form oven and cool for a few minutes.

8. Serve warm or room temperature.

stevia, raw honey or agave nectar

Carrot Cake Cookies

Prep Time: 10 minutes

Cook Time: 20 minutes

Servings: 12

INGREDIENTS

2 cups almond meal

4 large carrots (2 cups shredded)

3 eggs

1/4 cup coconut oil

1/3 cup unsweetened applesauce

1/2 cup coconut flakes

1/4 cup pitted dates

2 teaspoons vanilla

2 teaspoons ground cinnamon

1 teaspoon ground nutmeg

1 teaspoon ground ginger

INSTRUCTIONS

1. Preheat your oven to 350 Degrees F. Line sheet pan with parchment sheet or coat lightly with coconut oil.
2. Grate carrots, or process in food processor or bullet blender until finely chopped. Add to medium bowl.
3. Add eggs, oil, applesauce and dates to food processor or bullet blender. Process until thick, slightly chunky mixture forms. Pour into carrots.

4. Sift in almond meal. Then add spices and vanilla. Mix well with a wooden spoon. Stir in coconut.

5. Form 12 round balls and evenly space on sheet pan. Flatten balls with hand.

6. Bake about 20 minutes, or until firm and golden brown.

7. Remove from oven and allow to cool about 5 minutes.

8. Serve warm or room temperature.

raw honey, agave nectar or maple syrup

Chocolate Almond Biscotti

Prep Time: 15 minutes

Cook Time: 35* minutes

Servings: 6

INGREDIENTS

1 cup almond flour

1/2 cup coconut flour

1/2 cup sweetener*

1/3 cup almonds

2 tablespoons cocoa powder

1 teaspoon vanilla

1/2 teaspoon baking soda

1/4 teaspoon sea salt

INSTRUCTIONS

1. Preheat oven to 350 degrees F. Line sheet pan with parchment paper. Heat medium pan over medium heat.

2. Add almonds to hot dry pan and toast for about 5 minutes, until aromatic. Stir frequently. Remove from heat and set aside.

3. In medium mixing bowl, blend almond flour, coconut flour, cocoa powder, baking soda and salt with hand mixer or whisk.

4. Beat in sweetener and vanilla until well combined and thick, sticky dough forms. Mix in toasted almonds with wooden spoon.

5. Form dough into flattened, uniform mound about 1 inch thick on sheet pan. Pat down mound to keep any almonds from sticking out.

6. Bake for about 15 minutes . Remove and allow to cool for about 15 minutes.

7. Use a very sharp serrated knife to carefully cut biscotti log into 1/2 - 2/3 inch slices. Hold onto the mound and cut on a diagonal. If it becomes crumbly, stick it back together.

8. Lace slice on sides and return to oven for 15 minutes.

9. Try to cut so that you're holding on to the edges of the log to keep it from crumbling. If parts come apart, you can stick them back together as the mixture is still kind of sticky.

10. Lay the biscotti flat and return to oven for 15 minutes.

11. *Turn oven off and leave oven door open a crack. Allow the biscotti to cool and dry for at least 2 hours.

12. Serve room temperature.

*raw honey, agave nectar, maple syrup, or any combination

Chocolate Mousse

Prep Time: 5 minutes

Cook Time: 5 minutes

Servings: 2

INGREDIENTS

1 3/4 cups (about 2 cans) full-fat coconut milk

1 avocado

1/3 cup sweetener*

2 tablespoons cocoa powder

1 teaspoon vanilla

Handful cacao nibs or chapped nuts (optional)

INSTRUCTIONS

1. Process coconut milk, sweetener, cacao powder and vanilla in food processor or bullet blender until well combined.
2. Slice avocado in half and pit. Scoop flesh into mixture. Process until thick and creamy.
3. Stir in *optional* cacao nibs, nuts, etc.
4. Pour into ramekins or dessert cups and serve immediately. Or refrigerate for 1 hour to thicken.
5. Serve room temperature or chilled.

raw honey, agave nectar or maple syrup

Vanilla Pudding

Prep Time: 5 minutes

Cook Time: 10 minutes

Servings: 2

INGREDIENTS

13 oz (1 can) coconut milk

2 egg yolks

3 tablespoons sweetener*

2 tablespoons cacao butter

1 tablespoon vanilla

INSTRUCTIONS

1. Add coconut milk, sweetener and cacao butter to small pot and place over medium heat. Bring to a simmer, stirring periodically. Add vanilla.

2. In small mixing bowl, whisk 1 tablespoon hot coconut milk into egg yolks. Add second tablespoon. Slowly whisk in 1/4 cup of hot liquid, then add yolk mixture back to hot coconut milk.

3. Whisk custard constantly until thickened, about 5 minutes. Do not let pudding burn.

4. Pour hot pudding into ramekins or dessert cups and refrigerate at least 1 hour.

5. Once chilled, serve immediately. Or remove from fridge, and allow to warm up about 10 minutes and serve room temperature.

raw honey or agave nectar

Frozen Chocolate Cherry Custard

Prep Time: 15* minutes

Cook Time: 20 minutes

Servings: 4

INGREDIENTS

13 oz (1 can) full-fat coconut milk

3 oz water

5 egg yolks

1/4 cup sweetener*

1/2 cup pitted cherries

3 tablespoons cocoa powder

2 teaspoons vanilla

INSTRUCTIONS

1. *Freeze ice cream maker canister overnight before to make sure it is cold enough.

2. Heat coconut milk and water in medium pan over medium heat.

3. Slice cherries in half and set aside.

4. While milk is warmed, but not hot, whisk in egg yolks, sweetener and vanilla. Blend well.

5. Sift in cocoa powder and continue whisking until thickened, about 5 minutes.

6. Turn on ice cream maker first, then carefully pour in custard as ice cream maker paddle rotates.

7. Add halved cherries as ice cream maker runs.

8. Freeze mixture about 15 - 20 minutes. Then transfer frozen custard to serving dishes.

9. Serve immediately.

stevia, raw honey, agave nectar or maple syrup

Ginger Mango Sherbet

Prep Time: 5* minutes

Cook Time: 15 minutes

Servings: 4

INGREDIENTS

1 cup almond milk

1 cup coconut milk

2 ripe mangos

2 oz fresh ginger juice (about 8 inch bunch ginger root)

Juice of lime half

Zest of lime half

1 teaspoon vanilla

Bunch fresh mint

INSTRUCTIONS

1. *Freeze ice cream maker canister overnight before to make sure it is cold enough.
2. Add whole peeled ginger root to food processor. Or juice ginger and add to medium mixing bowl. Add mint leaves.
3. Slice, pit and peel mangos. Add to food processor or bullet blender with almond milk. Blend or process until smooth, then strain into medium mixing bowl.
4. Add coconut milk, juice and zest of half a lime, and vanilla. Mix well with whisk or hand mixer.
5. Turn on ice cream maker first, then carefully pour in mango mixture as ice cream maker paddle rotates.

6. Freeze for about 15 - 20 minutes. Then transfer frozen custard to serving dishes.

7. Serve immediately.

Sweet Potato Gnocchi

Prep Time: 20 minutes

Cook Time: 10 minutes

Servings: 2

INSTRUCTIONS

Gnocchi

1 large sweet potato

Pinch sea Salt

1 eggs

1 - 2 cups almond flour

1 - 2 cups tapioca flour (or arrowroot powder)

2 teaspoons ground cinnamon

1 teaspoon ground nutmeg

Sauce

1/4 cup pecans

1/4 cup sweetener* (or 1/4 cup dried pitted dates)

1/4 cup full-fat coconut milk

1 teaspoon vanilla

INGREDIENTS

1. Bring medium pot of lightly salted water to boil.
2. Peel, dice and boil sweet potatoes for about 5 - 10 minutes, until soft.
3. Drain sweet potatoes in colander and add to medium mixing bowl. Mash with hand mixer or whisk. Beat in eggs, salt and spices.

4. Bring medium pot of water to boil.

5. Beat 1/2 cup almond flour into sweet potato mixture. Alternate with 1/2 cup tapioca flour or arrowroot powder until dough you can roll in your hand forms. It will still be wet and slightly sticky.

6. Dust cutting board with a few tablespoons of almond flour and tapioca or arrowroot.

7. Roll a portion of dough into a snake about 1 inch thick. Slice roll into pieces 1/2 - 2/3 inch wide. Repeat with remaining dough.

8. Add gnocchi to boiling water in small batches. Cook until they float. Remove from water with slotted spoon or handled strainer and set aside.

9. Heat small pan over medium heat and add pecans. Toast about 2 minutes, then add coconut milk and vanilla. Stir in sweetener, or diced dates.

10. Add gnocchi to the pan and cook another minute or two.

11. Serve hot.

* stevia, raw honey, agave nectar or maple syrup

Flourless Chocolate Cake

Prep Time: 15 minutes

Cook Time: 30 minutes

Servings: 8

INGREDIENTS

16 oz organic bittersweet chocolate

1/4 cup cocoa powder

6 eggs

1 cup coconut oil

3/4 cup sweetener*

2 tablespoons water

2 teaspoons vanilla

1/4 teaspoon sea salt

INSTRUCTIONS

1. Preheat oven to 275 degrees F. Coat 2 mini spring form pans with coconut oil, then dust with cocoa powder, and cover the outside base of the pans with aluminum foil. Or line muffin pan with paper liners, or leave bare and coat liners or bare pan with coconut oil and dust with cocoa powder.

2. Slowly melt chocolate and coconut oil over a double boiler, heated over medium heat. Do not boil water in bottom of double boiler. Stir frequently.

3. Remove from heat once chocolate is melted and beat in sweetener, water, vanilla, salt and any remaining cocoa powder with hand mixer or whisk.

4. Beat in eggs one at a time until thoroughly incorporated.

5. Pour batter into vessels and bake for about 25 - 30 minutes, until set. Cakes will still appear a bit glossy and wet in the middle.

6. Cool for 30 minutes, then refrigerate at least 2 hours before serving.

7. Cut springform cakes with a knife warmed until hot running water, then dried.

8. Serve chilled or room temperature.

*maple syrup, raw honey or agave nectar

Apple Dump Muffins

Prep Time: 15 minutes

Cook Time: 25 minutes

Servings: 12

INGREDIENTS

6 medium apples

1 cup almond flour

1/4 cup tapioca flour

3 eggs

1/2 cup coconut oil

1/2 cup sweetener*

2 teaspoons baking powder

2 tablespoons ground cinnamon

1 teaspoon ground nutmeg

1 teaspoon sea salt

1/2 teaspoon black pepper (or white pepper)

Juice of lemon half

INSTRUCTIONS

1. Preheat oven to 350 degrees F. Lightly coat muffin pan with coconut oil, or line with paper liners.

2. Peel, core and thinly slice apples. Add to medium bowl with 1 tablespoon cinnamon and juice of half a lemon. Evenly sprinkle on tapioca flour and carefully toss with hands to coat apples.

3. In medium mixing bowl, blend almond flour, baking powder, spices and salt. Beat in eggs, sweetener and coconut oil with hand mixer or whisk. Fold in sliced apples.

4. Scoop batter into muffin pan and bake for 20 -25 minutes, or until top is browned and firm but springy. A toothpick inserted into the center should come our moist but clean.

5. Serve warm solo, or drizzled with your favorite sweetener.

NOTE: For *Apple Dump Cake*, bake in square baking dish or Bundt pan for 40 - 50 minutes.

raw honey, agave nectar or maple syrup

Pumpkin Spice Cakes

Prep Time: 5 minutes

Cook Time: 15 minutes

Servings: 12

INGREDIENTS

3/4 cup coconut flour

4 eggs

1/4 cup coconut oil

1/2 cup sweetener*

1/2 cup pumpkin purée

1 teaspoon baking soda

1 tablespoon ground cinnamon

1 tablespoon ground ginger

1 tablespoon ground nutmeg

1 tablespoon ground black pepper

1 teaspoon vanilla

1/2 teaspoon sea salt

1/4 cup pumpkin seeds

INSTRUCTIONS

1. Preheat oven to 350 degrees F. Lightly coat 4 mini cake pans or mini loaf pans with coconut oil, or line with parchment paper.

2. Sift coconut flour, baking soda, salt and spices into large mixing bowl.

3. In medium mixing bowl, beat egg whites to soft peaks with hand mixer or whisk. About 5 minutes.

4. Then beat in yolks, oil, sweetener and pumpkin purée. Mix wet ingredients into dry blend until combined.

5. Pour batter into mini cake loaf pans and sprinkle on pumpkin seeds.

6. Bake for 20 - 25 minutes, or until firm but springy in the center and browned. A toothpick inserted into the middle should come out clean.

7. Remove from oven and allow to cool for 5 minutes before serving.

8. Serve warm or room temperature.

NOTE: For large **Pumpkin Spice Cake**, oil large loaf pan or springform pan and bake 40 - 45 minutes.

raw honey, agave nectar or maple syrup

Fruit And Nut Cake

Prep Time: 10 minutes

Cook Time: 25 minutes

Servings: 8

INGREDIENTS

1 1/2 cup almond flour

4 eggs

2 tablespoons coconut oil

Juice of orange half

1/4 cup sweetener*

1/2 cup walnuts

1/4 cup pecans

1/2 cup dried pitted dates

1/2 cup dried cherries

1/4 cup dried apricots

1/4 cup raisins

1/2 teaspoon baking soda

1 teaspoon ground ginger

1 teaspoon vanilla

1/2 teaspoon sea salt

Zest of orange half

INSTRUCTIONS

1. Preheat oven to 350 degrees F. Lightly coat 2 small loaf pans or one Bundt pan with coconut oil.
2. Sift almond flour, baking soda and salt into large mixing bowl.

3. Chop walnuts, pecans, apricots and dates. Then stir all dried fruit and nuts into flour mixture.

4. In medium mixing bowl, mix eggs, coconut oil, juice and zest of half an orange, sweetener, ginger and vanilla. Then pour and mix into dry ingredients until just combined.

5. Scoop batter into loaf pans or Bundt pan, and smooth tops with spatula.

6. Bake 20 - 30 minutes, or until firm, browned and firm in the center.

7. Remove from oven and allow to cool before slicing.

8. Serve warm or room temperature.

*stevia, raw honey or agave nectar

Toasted Almond Cream Cakes

Prep Time: 15 minutes*

Cook Time: 20 minutes

Servings: 12

INGREDIENTS

Cake

1 cup almond flour

4 egg whites

1/3 cup coconut oil

1/4 cup almond milk

1/4 cup sweetener*

1 teaspoon baking powder

1/4 cup slice almonds

Almond Cream

2 cups skinless almonds

1/4 cup sweetener

1 teaspoon vanilla

Water

INSTRUCTIONS

1. *Soak almonds overnight in water. Drain and rinse.
2. Preheat the oven to 350 degrees F. Heat medium pan over medium heat. Lightly coat muffin pan with coconut oil, or line with paper liners

3. Add almond flour to hot dry pan and toast about 5 minutes, stirring frequently. Do not burn. Remove from heat and set aside.

4. Beat egg whites to soft peaks with hand mixer or whisk in medium bowl. Then beat in oil, milk and 1/4 cup sweetener. Sift in toasted almond flour and baking powder. Mix until just combined.

5. Use ice cream scoop or spoon to scoop batter into muffin pan. Each cup should be only 1/2 full.

6. Bake about 15 minutes, or until center is set but springy.

7. Remove pan from oven and remove cakes from pan. Let cool for about 15 minutes.

8. While cakes cool, blend soaked almonds, 1/4 cup sweetener, 1 teaspoon vanilla and water as needed in food processor or blender to make smooth *Almond Cream*.

9. Wipe out pan with paper towel and return dry pan to medium heat. Toast slice almonds about 5 minutes, until aromatic and golden. Do not burn. Remove from heat and set aside.

10. When cakes are cooled, slice in half to create top and bottom layer. Scoop cream onto bottom half, and top with top half of cake. Scoop another dollop of cream over top half and sprinkle on slice toasted almonds.

11. Serve room temperature.

NOTE: For large **Toasted Almond Cream Cake** , bake batter in 2 round cake pans for 35 - 40 minutes.

raw honey, agave nectar or maple syrup

Pineapple Upside Down Cake

Prep Time: 15 minutes

Cook Time: 30 minutes

Servings: 12

INGREDIENTS

2 cups almond flour

8 - 12 slices organic canned pineapple in juice

8 - 12 pitted cherries

1/4 cup sweetener*

3 eggs

1/4 cup coconut oil

1/2 cup organic pineapple juice (reserved from can)

2 teaspoons baking soda

2 teaspoons vanilla

1/2 teaspoon sea salt

INSTRUCTIONS

1. Preheat oven to 350 degrees F. Line 9x13 baking dish with parchment paper, or coat with coconut oil.

2. Arrange pineapple slices and cherries on bottom of baking dish. Place in oven while you prepare the batter.

3. Beat egg whites to stiff peaks with hand mixer or whisk in medium mixing bowl. About 7 - 10 minutes.

4. In large mixing bowl, mix yolks, olive oil, sweetener, pineapple juice and vanilla.

5. Sift almond flour, baking soda and salt into yolk mixture. Beat until well combined.

6. Fold egg whites into batter until evenly combined.

7. Remove hot baking pan from oven, and spread light batter over pineapple and cherries. Smooth top with spatula.

8. Bake for 25 - 30 minutes, or until cake golden brown and firm but springy in the center. A toothpick inserted into the center should come out clean.

9. Remove pan from oven and allow to cool for 15 minutes. Turn cake out onto serving dish and remove parchment. Or scrape any stuck fruit from the pan and place back on cake.

10. Allow to cool another 15 minutes before serving. Serve room temperature or warm.

NOTE: For **Pineapple Upside Dow Cupcakes** , add a pineapple slice and cherry to muffin pan lined with paper liners or coated with coconut oil, then fill cups 2/3 full with batter and bake about 20 minutes.

stevia, raw honey or agave nectar

Baking Recipes

Introduction

Welcome to the recipe book that will guide you through baking great-tasting goods that are not only wheat-free, but naturally sweetened. That means none of these baked goods will contain, or even need, refined sugars. Enjoy sweeteners made from Mother Nature herself, including raw honey and agave nectar. All of the ingredients come from fresh, whole foods that have not undergone any processing. Processed and refined foods as well as wheat, have been linked to health problems for increasing amounts of people. When removing them from the diet, research has shown a decrease in blood sugar instability, cholesterol, obesity and digestion problems. Baking has never tasted or felt so good!

Nourish your body and satisfy that nagging sweet tooth with these delicious baked goods. Your kids, friends and coworkers will not believe that these indulgences are actually healthy. Shh....maybe don't tell the kids! Transform your thinking of a wheat-free diet from a limitation, to the opportunity that it is. Try new dishes, nourish your body and lose a couple pesky extra pounds with these delicious baking recipes. Grab your oven mitts and get ready to try these mouth-watering dishes you won't be able to keep to yourself.

Table of Contents

Mocha Brownie Bites
Blueberry Scones
Double Pumpkin Muffins
Cinnamon Raisin Bread
Quick Sandwich Rolls
Classic Bagels
All-Purpose Pizza Crust
Plain Pita
Sesame Pretzel Sticks
Breakfast Buns
Avocado Club Muffin
Chicken Dumpling Bun
Easy Poppy Seed Muffins
Coconut Macaroons
Blackberry Dumplings
Carrot Cake Cookie Bars
Sugar-Free Coconut Cake
Chocolate Zucchini Cake
Apple Pastries
Cocoa Cream Muffins
Ginger Spice Cookies
Lemon Coconut Bars
Sweet Potato Cinnamon Rolls

Candied Banana Bread
Orange Cranberry Muffins

Mocha Brownie Bites

Prep Time: 5 minutes

Cook Time: 25 minutes

Servings: 16

INGREDIENTS

4 cage-free eggs

1 cup cocoa powder

1/4 cup coconut oil

1/4 cup full-fat coconut milk

1/4 cup sweetener*

2 teaspoons instant espresso (or instant coffee)

1 teaspoon vanilla

INSTRUCTIONS

14. Preheat oven to 350 degrees F. Lightly oil square baking dish or line with parchment.

15. Add eggs, coconut oil, coconut milk and sweetener to medium mixing bowl and beat with hand mixer or whisk. Sift in cocoa powder, espresso and vanilla. Beat until well combined.

16. Pour batter into prepared baking pan and bake for 20 - 25 minutes, until set.

17. Allow to cool completely.

18. Slice and serve room temperature. Or refrigerate and serve chilled.

raw honey, agave nectar or maple syrup

Blueberry Scones

Prep Time: 5 minutes

Cook Time: 25 minutes

Servings: 8

INGREDIENTS

2 cups almond flour

1/3 cup arrowroot powder (or tapioca flour)

1 cage-free egg

1/2 cup dried or frozen blueberries

1/4 cup coconut oil

2 tablespoons sweetener*

2 teaspoons baking powder

1/2 teaspoon vanilla

1/2 teaspoon sea salt

1/4 teaspoon ground cinnamon (optional)

INSTRUCTIONS

6. Preheat oven to 350 degrees F. Line sheet pan with parchment or coat with coconut oil.

7. Whisk together almond flour, arrowroot powder, baking powder, salt, vanilla and cinnamon (optional) in medium mixing bowl.

8. In small mixing bowl, beat egg, oil and sweetener with hand mixer or whisk. Add egg mixture to dry ingredients and mix until well combined.

9. Fold in blueberries. Form dough into ball and place on sheet pan . Pat down to flatten to about 1/2 inch thick circle.

10. Cut into eight wedges with pizza cutter or sharp knife. Arrange at least 1 inch apart on sheet pan and bake for 20 - 25 minutes , or until edges are golden brown.

11. Remove from oven and let cool at least 10 minutes.

12. Serve room temperature.

raw honey, agave nectar or grade B maple syrup

Double Pumpkin Muffins

Prep Time: 5 minutes

Cook Time: 25 minutes

Servings: 12

INGREDIENTS

1 3/4 cups coconut flour

2 cage-free eggs

15 oz (1 can) organic pumpkin puree

1 cup unsweetened applesauce

1/2 cup coconut oil

1/4 cup sweetener*

2 teaspoons baking soda

1 1/2 tablespoon ground cinnamon

1/2 teaspoon ground nutmeg

1 teaspoon sea salt

1/2 cup pumpkin seeds

INSTRUCTIONS

8. Preheat oven to 350 degrees F. Line muffin pan with paper liner or coat with coconut oil.

9. Process eggs, coconut oil, applesauce and sweetener in food processor or blender until thick and light, about 2 minutes.

10. Pour egg mixture into medium mixing bowl. Add pumpkin puree, salt and spices and mix with hand mixer or whisk.

11. Sift in coconut flour and baking soda. Mix until well combined. Stir in half of pumpkin seeds.

12. Pour batter into prepared muffin pan and sprinkle remaining pumpkin seeds over batter.

13. Place in oven and bake 20 - 25 minutes , until edges are golden and tops firm but springy.

14. Remove from oven and allow to cool 5 minutes.

15. Serve warm. Or let cool complete and serve room temperature.

stevia, raw honey or agave nectar

Cinnamon Raisin Bread

Prep Time: 5 minutes

Cook Time: 20 minutes

Servings: 12

INGREDIENTS

3/4 cup coconut flour

3/4 cup almond flour

1/4 cup ground chia seed (or flax meal)

2 cage-free eggs

1/2 cup raisins

1/2 cup coconut oil

1/2 cup unsweetened applesauce

1/4 cup sweetener*

2 tablespoons ground cinnamon

1 teaspoon baking powder

1 teaspoon sea salt

1/2 teaspoon ground black pepper (optional)

INSTRUCTIONS

1. Preheat oven to 350 degrees F. Line baking pan with parchment or coat with coconut oil.

2. In large bowl, whisk eggs with hand mixer or whisk until frothy and light. Add coconut oil, sweetener and applesauce. Blend until combined.

3. Sift coconut and almond flour, chia meal, baking powder, salt and spices into wet ingredients. Beat until smooth and well combined. Stir in raisins.

4. Pour batter into prepared baking pan.

5. Bake for 20 - 25 minutes, or until golden brown and firm to the touch.

6. Remove from oven and let cool about 5 minutes.

7. Slice and serve warm. Or allow to cool completely and serve room temperature.

NOTE: Bake in oiled loaf pan for 40 - 45 minutes for **Cinnamon Raison Bread** loaf.

stevia, raw honey or agave nectar

Quick Sandwich Rolls

Prep Time: 5 minutes

Cook Time: 25 minutes

Servings: 4

INGREDIENTS

Sandwich Rolls

1 cup tapioca flour

1/4 - 1/3 cup coconut flour

1 cage-free egg

1/2 cup warm water

1/4 cup coconut oil

1/4 cup unsweetened applesauce

1 teaspoon apple cider vinegar

1/2 teaspoon baking soda

3/4 teaspoon sea salt

INSTRUCTIONS

6. Preheat oven to 350 degrees F. Line sheet pan with parchment paper or coat with coconut oil. Or coat 4 round mini cake pans with coconut oil.

7. Warm 1/2 cup water in small pot over medium heat.

8. In medium bowl, blend tapioca flour, 1/4 cup coconut flour, baking soda and salt.

9. Add 1 egg, applesauce and coconut oil to food processor or bullet blender. Process about 30 seconds, until a bit light and frothy.

10. Add egg mixture and warm water to flour mixture. Mix until well combined.

11. add coconut flour or water 1 tablespoon at a time to form a soft and slightly sticky dough, if necessary,.

12. Divide dough into 4 portions and roll into round or oblong balls. Dust your hand with extra tapioca flour to prevent sticking.

13. Place rolls on prepared sheet pan and pat down slightly. Brush tops with coconut oil, if preferred.

14. Bake about 25 minutes, or until edges are golden brown and tops are firm.

15. Remove from oven and let cool at least 10 minutes.

16. Slice in half, fill with your favorite cold cuts or hot meats, and serve.

Classic Bagels

Prep Time: 10 minutes

Cook Time: 25 minutes

Servings: 8

INGREDIENTS

2 cups almond flour

2 tablespoons coconut flour

2 tablespoons ground chia seed (or flax meal)

1 tablespoon tapioca flour (or arrowroot powder)

4 cage-free eggs

1/3 cup apple cider vinegar

2 tablespoons unsweetened applesauce

2 tablespoons sweetener*

1 teaspoon baking soda

1/2 teaspoon sea salt

INSTRUCTIONS

6. Preheat oven to 350 degrees. Lightly coat donut pan with coconut oil.

7. Add almond, coconut and tapioca flours, chia meal, baking soda and salt to food processor or bullet blender, and process for 1 minute.

8. Add eggs, sweetener, applesauce and apple cider vinegar to flour mixture and process until fully blended, about 1 - 2 minutes.

9. Carefully scoop batter into donut pan, avoiding raised middle.

10. Place in oven and bake about 20 - 25 minutes.

11. Remove and let cool about 5 minutes. Then remove from pan.

12. Slice in half and serve immediately. Or let cool completely and serve room temperature.

NOTE: Bake in 8 round mini cake pans lightly coated with coconut oil if you do not have a donut pan.

stevia, raw honey or agave nectar

All-Purpose Pizza Crust

Prep Time: 5 minutes

Cook Time: 20 minutes

Servings: 2

INGREDIENTS

1/3 cup coconut flour

3 cage-free eggs

1/2 cup coconut milk

2 tablespoons flax meal (or ground chia seed)

2 tablespoons tapioca flour

1 teaspoon baking powder

1/2 teaspoon sea salt

INSTRUCTIONS

1. Preheat oven to 350 degrees F. Line sheet pan with parchment paper or baking mat, or coat lightly with coconut oil.
2. In medium bowl, beat eggs and coconut milk with hand mixer or whisk until well combined.
3. Sift coconut and tapioca flour, flax meal, baking powder and salt into egg mixture. Beat into thick batter.
4. Spread batter into desired shape on sheet pan with ladle or spatula.
5. Place in oven and bake for 10 minutes, or until firm enough to flip.
6. Carefully remove par baked crust. Peel away from sheet pan and turn over.
7. Return crust to oven and bake for additional 8 - 10 minutes, or until cooked through.

8. Remove crust and evenly spread with desired sauce and sprinkle with favorite toppings.

9. Set oven to broil. Broil pizza for 1 - 2 minutes, just to heat toppings.

10. Remove pizza and slice with knife or pizza cutter. Serve hot.

Plain Pita

Prep Time: 5 minutes

Cook Time: 20 minutes

Servings: 1

INGREDIENTS

1 cup tapioca flour

1 cage-free egg

1/4 cup water

2 tablespoons coconut oil

1 teaspoon ground chia seed (or flax meal)

1/2 teaspoon baking soda

1/4 teaspoon ground white pepper (or black pepper)

1/4 teaspoon sea salt

INSTRUCTIONS

1. Preheat the oven to 375 degrees F. Line sheet pan with parchment paper or baking mat, or lightly coat with coconut oil. Heat small pot over low heat.
2. Add 1/3 cup tapioca flour, chia meal, water and 1 tablespoon coconut oil to pot. Stir until mixture comes together. Remove from heat and cool in freezer.
3. In medium bowl, blend remaining tapioca flour, baking soda, salt and pepper. Then add egg and remaining oil. Mix until combined.
4. Add cooled chia mixture to bowl. Mix to combine, then remove and knead briefly to bring together dough.

5. Form round disk, then flatten on prepared sheet pan to 1/4 - 1/3 inch with hands or rolling pin.

6. Place in oven and bake about 15 minutes. Carefully remove pan and turn pita over with spatula. Return to oven and bake another 5 - 10 minutes, or until crisp.

7. Remove from oven and fill with favorite Mediterranean meats. Or cut into wedges and dip into favorite spreads.

8. Serve warm or room temperature.

Sesame Pretzel Sticks

Prep Time: 15 minutes

Cook Time: 20 minutes

Servings: 6

INGREDIENTS

1 cup coconut flour

1/2 cup tapioca flour

1/3 cup coconut oil

2 tablespoons unsweetened applesauce

1/2 cup water

1 cage-free egg

2 tablespoons apple cider vinegar

1/2 teaspoon baking soda

1/2 teaspoon baking powder

1/2 teaspoon sea salt

1 tablespoon sesame seeds

INSTRUCTIONS

1. Preheat oven to 350 degrees F. Heat medium pan over medium-high heat. Line sheet pan with parchment or baking mat.
2. Add coconut oil, water, vinegar and salt to pot. Bring to a boil and remove from heat. Stir in apple sauce.
3. Whisk in tapioca flour. Stir with wooden spoon or soft spatula until mixture gels and comes together.

4. Stir in baking soda and baking powder. Continue mixing for about 1 minute. Mixture will foam and expand. Let mixture sit and cool about 5 minutes.

5. Sift in coconut flour. Mix partially, then beat in egg. Blend until combined. Excess coconut flour may sit in bottom of bowl.

6. Turn out dough onto cutting board dusted with any excess coconut flour from mixture. Knead dough for 2 minutes.

7. Cut dough into 6 equal portions. Roll out pieces into ropes, then lay straight on prepared sheet pan. Use knife to score dough diagonally a few times for presentation.

8. Brush with coconut oil or full-fat coconut milk and sprinkle with sesame seeds.

9. Place sheet pan in oven and bake about 20 - 25 minutes, until cooked through.

10. Serve immediately with favorite dipping sauce. Or allow to cool and serve room temperature.

Breakfast Buns

Prep Time: 15 minutes

Cook Time: 20 minutes

Servings: 4

INGREDIENTS

Breakfast Bun

1 cup tapioca flour

1/4 - 1/3 cup coconut flour

1 cage-free egg

1/2 cup warm water

1/4 cup coconut oil

Bacon drippings

2 tablespoons applesauce

1 teaspoon apple cider vinegar

1/2 teaspoon baking soda

1/2 teaspoon ground black pepper

1/4 teaspoon sea salt

Filling

4 cage-free eggs

4 slices nitrate-free bacon

1/2 small bell pepper

1/2 small onion

1/4 teaspoon ground black pepper

1/4 teaspoon sea salt

INSTRUCTIONS

1. Preheat oven to 350 degrees F. Line sheet pan with parchment paper or coat with coconut oil. Heat medium skillet over medium-high heat. Add water to small pot and heat over medium heat.

2. For *Filling*, peel onion, stem, seed and vein pepper, and chop bacon. Add bacon to hot skillet and sauté until bacon is crisp and almost cooked through. Drain off drippings and set aside.

3. Dice onion and pepper and add to bacon. Sauté about 2 minutes, unto bacon is cooked through and veggies are softened. Add eggs and lightly scrambled, just 30 seconds - 1 minute. Remove from heat and set aside.

4. For *Breakfast Bun*, sift together tapioca flour, coconut flour, baking soda, salt and pepper in medium bowl.

5. Whisk egg, applesauce and vinegar in small bowl. Whisk in warm water, coconut oil and bacon drippings.

6. Add egg mixture to flour mixture and mix until well combined. Add 1 tablespoon coconut flour or water at a time if needed to form soft and slightly sticky dough.

7. Divide dough into 4 portions and flatten into round disks. Dust your hand or rolling pin with extra tapioca flour to prevent sticking.

8. Scoop loose egg *Filling* into center of each dough disk and pinch edges of dough together to create round, sealed ball.

9. Place filled buns sealed side down on sheet pan and pat down slightly.

10. Place in oven and bake 20 minutes, or until edges are golden brown and dough is cooked through.

11. Remove from oven and let cool about 5 minutes.

12. Serve warm.

Avocado Club Muffin

Prep Time: 10 minutes

Cook Time: 15 minutes

Servings: 12

INGREDIENTS

1 cup almond flour

2 cage-free eggs

1 avocado

4 slices nitrate-free bacon

1 tablespoon sweetener*

1 teaspoon apple cider vinegar

1 teaspoon baking powder

1/4 teaspoon ground white pepper (or black pepper)

INSTRUCTIONS

1. Preheat oven to 350 degrees F. Line muffin pan with paper liners or light coat with coconut oil. Heat medium pan over medium-high heat.

2. Finely chop bacon and add to hot pan. Sauté until crisp and cooked through, about 5 minutes. Set aside.

3. Beat eggs, sweetener and vinegar in medium mixing bowl with hand mixer or whisk until thick and slightly foamy.

4. Slice avocado in half. Scoop flesh of one half into egg mixture. Add bacon and drippings, almond flour, baking powder and black pepper and mix until combined.

5. Dice remaining avocado flesh and fold into batter.

6. Use ice cream scoop or tablespoon to scoop batter into prepared muffin pan.

7. Bake about 15 - 20 minutes, until edges are golden brown and tops are firm.

8. Remove from oven and let cool for 5 minutes.

9. Serve warm. Or cool completely and serve temperature.

NOTE: Bake in square oiled baking pan for 30 - 35 minutes for **Avocado Club Bread**.

stevia, raw honey or agave nectar

Chicken Dumpling Bun

Prep Time: 15 minutes

Cook Time: 20 minutes

Servings: 4

INGREDIENTS

Dumpling Bun

1 cup tapioca flour

1/4 - 1/3 cup coconut flour

1 cage-free egg

1/2 cup warm chicken stock

1/4 cup coconut oil

1/4 cup applesauce

1 teaspoon apple cider vinegar

1 teaspoon baking soda

1/2 teaspoon onion powder

1/ 4 teaspoon garlic powder

1/2 teaspoon sea salt

Filling

8 oz boneless chicken (breasts, thighs, etc.)

1 small carrot

1 small celery stalk

1/2 teaspoon dried thyme

1/4 teaspoon ground sage

1/2 teaspoon ground black pepper

1/2 teaspoon sea salt

INSTRUCTIONS

1. Preheat oven to 350 degrees F. Line sheet pan with parchment paper or coat with coconut oil. Heat medium skillet over medium heat and lightly coat with coconut oil.

2. Add chicken stock to small pot and heat over medium heat.

3. For *Filling*, dice carrot and celery, fillet chicken in half, and add to hot oiled skillet with salt and spices. Sauté until chicken is cooked through and browned and veggies are softened, about 5 - 8 minutes. Remove from heat and set aside. Shred or dice rested chicken and mix thoroughly with sautéed veggies.

4. For *Dumpling Bun*, sift together tapioca flour, coconut flour, baking soda, salt and spices in medium bowl.

5. Whisk egg, applesauce and vinegar in small bowl. Whisk in warm chicken stock and coconut oil.

6. Add egg mixture to flour mixture and mix until well combined. Add 1 tablespoon coconut flour or water at a time if needed to form soft and slightly sticky dough.

7. Divide dough into 4 portions and flatten into round disks. Dust your hand or rolling pin with extra tapioca flour to prevent sticking.

8. Scoop chicken *Filling* into center of each dough disk and pinch edges of dough together to create round, sealed ball.

9. Place filled buns sealed side down on sheet pan and pat down slightly.

10. Place in oven and bake 20 minutes, or until edges are golden brown and dough is cooked through.

11. Remove from oven and let cool about 5 minutes.

12. Serve warm.

Easy Poppy Seed Muffins

Prep Time: 5 minutes

Cook Time: 20 minutes

Servings: 12

INGREDIENTS

6 eggs

1/2 cup coconut flour

1/4 cup coconut oil

1/4 cup sweetener*

1 teaspoon vanilla

1 teaspoon poppy seeds

1/2 teaspoon baking soda

Juice of 2 lemons

Zest of 2 lemons

INSTRUCTIONS

12. Preheat oven to 350 degrees F. Oil muffin pan or line with paper liners.

13. Zest, *then* juice 2 lemons. Add to large mixing bowl with eggs, coconut oil, sweetener and vanilla. Beat with hand mixer or whisk until well combined.

14. Sift coconut flour and baking soda into wet ingredients, and mix until smooth. Stir in poppy seeds.

15. Use ice cream scoop or tablespoon to pour batter into prepared muffin pan.

16. Place in oven and bake for about 20 minutes, or until golden around edges and toothpick inserted into middle comes out clean.

17. Remove from oven and let cool for 5 minutes.

18. Serve warm. Or allow to cool completely and serve room temperature.

* raw honey or agave nectar

Coconut Macaroons

Prep Time: 10 minutes

Cook Time: 20 minutes

Servings: 12

INGREDIENTS

6 cage-free egg whites

3 cups flaked coconut

1/2 cup sweetener*

1 tablespoon coconut oil

1 teaspoon vanilla

1/4 teaspoon sea salt

INSTRUCTIONS

11. Preheat oven to 350 degrees F. Line a sheet pan with parchment paper or baking mat.

12. In large mixing bowl, beat room temperature egg whites with hand mixer to stiff peaks, about 7 - 8 minutes.

13. Beat in sweetener, vanilla and salt until combined. Fold in 1 cup of coconut at a time.

14. Use ice cream scoop or spoon to drop rounds of batter onto prepared sheet pan.

15. Bake for about 20 minutes, or until coconut is toasted and browned.

16. Allow to cool on pan for 10 minutes. Then remove from pan.

17. Serve warm. Or allow to cool completely and serve room temperature.

raw honey or agave nectar

Blackberry Dumplings

Prep Time: 15 minutes

Cook Time: 20 minutes

Servings: 8

INGREDIENTS

Blackberry Filling

2 1/2 cups blackberries (fresh or frozen)

2 - 4 tablespoons sweetener*

2 tablespoons tapioca flour

1/2 teaspoon ground black pepper

Zest of 1/2 lemon

Dumplings

1/4 cup coconut flour

3/4 cup almond flour

3 tablespoons cold coconut oil

1 teaspoon baking powder

1/2 teaspoon ground cinnamon

1/4 teaspoon sea salt

2 cage-free eggs

2 tablespoon sweetener

1 teaspoon vanilla

Zest of 1/2 lemon

INSTRUCTIONS

1. For *Dumplings*, sift coconut flour, almond flour, baking powder and salt into small mixing bowl. Cut in cold coconut oil with fork until crumbly. Place in freezer for 10 minutes.

2. Preheat oven to 400 degrees F.

3. For *Blackberry Filling*, add blackberries, sweetener, black pepper and lemon zest to medium pot. Heat over medium heat and bring to simmer. Whisk in tapioca flour and simmer about 10 minutes.

4. Pour hot blackberries into casserole dish and place in hot oven.

5. In medium bowl, beat eggs, sweetener, lemon zest, cinnamon and vanilla. Add chilled flour mixture to eggs and mix until dough comes together.

6. Carefully remove dish from oven and drop 8 dumplings onto bubbling berries.

7. Return dish to oven and bake 15 - 20 min, until dumplings are golden, set and cooked through.

8. Remove dish from oven and allow to cool about 5 minutes.

9. Serve warm. Or allow to cool completely and serve room temperature.

*stevia, raw honey or agave nectar

Carrot Cake Cookie Bars

Prep Time: 10 minutes

Cook Time: 25 minutes

Servings: 12

INGREDIENTS

2 cups almond meal

2 cups shredded carrots (about 4 large carrots)

3 cage-free eggs

1/4 cup coconut oil

1/2 cup unsweetened applesauce

1/2 cup flaked coconut

1/4 cup sweetener*

2 teaspoons vanilla

2 teaspoons ground cinnamon

1 teaspoon ground nutmeg

1/2 teaspoon ground black pepper

1/2 teaspoon sea salt

INSTRUCTIONS

9. Preheat oven to 350 Degrees F. Line baking pan with parchment or coat lightly with coconut oil.

10. Grate carrots, or process in food processor or bullet blender until finely chopped. Add to medium bowl.

11. Add eggs, oil, applesauce and sweetener to food processor or bullet blender. Process until thickened and light, about 1 - 2 minutes.

12. Pour egg mixture into carrots. Sift in almond flour and salt. Add vanilla and spices. Mix well with a wooden spoon or hand mixer. Stir in coconut.

13. Press dough evenly into prepared baking pan and bake about 25 minutes, or until firm and golden brown.

14. Remove from oven and allow to cool about 10 minutes.

15. Slice into bars and serve warm. Or let cool completely and serve room temperature.

stevia, raw honey, agave nectar or maple syrup

Sugar-Free Coconut Cake

Prep Time: 10 minutes

Cook Time: 25 minutes

Servings: 12

INGREDIENTS

Coconut Cake

6 cage-free eggs

3/4 cup coconut flour

1 cup flaked coconut

1 cup unsweetened applesauce

1/2 cup coconut oil

1/2 cup coconut milk

1/2 cup sweetener*

1/2 cup dried pitted dates

2 teaspoons vanilla

1 teaspoon baking soda

1 teaspoon baking powder

1/2 teaspoon sea salt

Coconut Frosting

1/3 cup coconut cream (from 1 can settled full-fat coconut milk)

2 - 4 tablespoons sweetener*

1/2 teaspoon vanilla

1/2 cup flaked coconut

INSTRUCTIONS

1. Preheat oven to 325°F. Line two or square baking pans with parchment or coat lightly with coconut oil.

2. Add dates, coconut milk, and half of eggs and oil to food processor or bullet blender. Process until dates a broken down, about 1 - 2 minutes.

3. Pour date mixture into medium bowl. Add applesauce, sweetener, vanilla, and remaining eggs and oil. Beat with hand mixer or whisk until well combined.

4. Sift coconut flour, salt, and baking soda and baking powder into wet ingredients. Blend until smooth. Stir in coconut.

5. Pour batter into prepared baking pans and bake for about 25 minutes, or until golden and toothpick inserted into center comes out clean.

6. Remove from oven and allow to cool. Place in refrigerator to speed cooling.

7. For *Coconut Frosting*, beat coconut cream in medium mixing bowl until slightly thickened. Add sweetener and vanilla, and continue to beat until full thickened and fluffy.

8. Frost cooled cakes and stack one on top of the other. Evenly sprinkle flaked coconut on top layer of frosted cake.

9. Slice and serve.

*stevia, raw honey, agave nectar or maple syrup

Chocolate Zucchini Cake

Prep Time: 10 minutes

Cook Time: 25 minutes

Servings: 12

INGREDIENTS

1 1/2 cups almond flour

2 cage-free eggs

1 medium zucchini (1 1/2 cups grated)

1/2 cup unsweetened applesauce

1/4 cup coconut oil

1/4 - 1/2 cup sweetener*

1/4 cup cocoa powder

2 tablespoons ground chia seed (or flax meal)

1 teaspoon baking soda

1 teaspoon baking powder

1 teaspoon vanilla

1 teaspoon ground cinnamon

1 teaspoon ground black pepper

1/2 teaspoon sea salt

1/4 cup cocoa nibs or chocolate chips (optional)

INSTRUCTIONS

9. Preheat oven to 350 degrees F. Line rectangular baking pan with parchment or lightly coat with coconut oil.

10. Add eggs, coconut oil, applesauce and sweetener to food processor or bullet blender. Process until mixture is thick and lightened.

11. Grate zucchini and add to medium mixing bowl. Pour egg mixture over grated zucchini.

12. Sift almond flour, cocoa powder, chia meal, baking soda and powder, salt and spices into bowl. Beat with hand mixer or whisk to combine. Stir in cocoa nibs or chocolate chips (optional).

13. Pour batter into prepared baking pan and bake for about 25 minutes, until toothpick inserted into center comes out clean.

14. Remove from oven and let cool about 10 minutes.

15. Slice and serve warm. Or let cool completely and serve room temperature.

*stevia, raw honey or agave nectar

Apple Pastries

Prep Time: 20 minutes

Cook Time: 20 minutes

Servings: 4

INSTRUCTIONS

Crust

2 cups almond flour

2 cage-free eggs

3 tablespoons coconut oil

1 tablespoon sweetener*

1/2 teaspoon baking soda

1/2 teaspoon baking powder

1 teaspoon ground cinnamon

1/4 teaspoon sea salt

Filling

2 sweet apples

1/4 cup water

1 teaspoon tapioca flour

1 tablespoon ground cinnamon

1/2 teaspoon ground nutmeg

1 teaspoon vanilla

2 tablespoons sweetener * (optional)

2 tablespoons raisins (optional)

2 tablespoons chopped walnuts (optional)

DIRECTIONS

1. For *Crust*, sift almond flour into medium mixing bowl. Add baking soda and powder, cinnamon and salt.

2. Whisk eggs and sweetener in small mixing bowl, then add to flour mixture and combine. Slowly add coconut oil until malleable dough comes together.

3. Roll in plastic wrap or wrap tightly in parchment and refrigerate for 15 minutes.

4. Preheat oven to 400 degrees. Line sheet pan with parchment or baking mat. Cover cutting board with parchment. Heat medium pan over medium-high heat.

5. For *Filling*, peel and dice apples. Add apples to hot pan with water, tapioca, cinnamon, nutmeg, and sweetener and spices (optional).

6. Stir and simmer for about 5 - 8 minutes, until apples are tender and thick glaze forms. Remove from heat and add raisins and chopped walnuts (optional).

7. Remove dough from refrigerator. Roll dough out on parchment covered cutting board to about 1/8 inch thick square with rolling pin. Use sharp knife or pizza cutter to cut dough into 4 squares.

8. Scoop equal portions of *Filling* into center of one side of each dough square. Fold bare half of dough over filled half. Press edges together and secure seal, letting any trapped air escape. Repeat with remaining dough.

9. Arrange pies on lined sheet pan and bake 15 - 20 minutes, or until dough is golden and cooked through.

10. Serve immediately. Or allow to cool and serve room temperature.

*stevia, raw honey or agave nectar

Cocoa Cream Muffins

Prep Time: 10 minutes*

Cook Time: 20 minutes

Servings: 12

INGREDIENTS

1 cup almond flour

1 cup coconut flour

3 cage-free eggs

1/2 cup unsweetened applesauce

1/4 cup coconut oil

1/4 cup sweetener*

1 avocado

3 tablespoons cocoa powder

1 tablespoon baking powder

1/4 teaspoon ground black pepper

1 teaspoon sea salt

Filling

2 cups water

1 cup cashews

3 tablespoons sweetener*

2 tablespoon cocoa powder

2 - 4 tablespoons coconut milk

INSTRUCTIONS

8. *Soak cashews overnight in 2 cups water. Drain and rinse. Set aside.

9. Preheat oven to 350 degrees F. Line muffin pan with paper liners or coat with coconut oil.

10. Slice avocado in half, pit, and scoop flesh into food processor or blender. Add eggs, coconut oil, applesauce and sweetener. Process until smooth.

11. Pour avocado blend into medium mixing bowl. Sift in almond flour, cocoa powder, baking powder, salt and pepper. Beat with hand mixer or whisk until combined.

12. Pour batter into prepared muffin pan. Bake 20 -25 minutes, or until firm but springy in center.

13. For *Filling*, add soaked cashews, sweetener and cocoa powder to food processor or bullet blender. Process until smooth and creamy. Add coconut milk if necessary to reach desired consistency.

14. Remove muffins from oven and let cool.

15. Scoop out center of muffin with knife or teaspoon, and fill with *Filling*. Or transfer *Filling* to pastry bag fitted with 1/2 inch tip, insert tip into muffin and fill.

16. Serve warm or room temperature.

*stevia, raw honey or agave nectar

Ginger Spice Cookies

Prep Time: 15 minutes

Cook Time: 15 minutes

Servings: 6

INGREDIENTS

1 1/2 cups almond flour

1 cage-free egg

1/4 cup sweetener*

2 tablespoons coconut oil

1 teaspoon ground chia seed (or flax meal)

1/4 teaspoon baking soda

1 tablespoon ground ginger

1/2 teaspoon ground clove

Pinch all spice

Pinch ground black pepper

Pinch sea salt

INSTRUCTIONS

1. Preheat oven to 350 degrees F. Line sheet pan with parchment or baking mat, or lightly coat with coconut oil.
2. Beat egg, oil, sweetener and chia meal in medium mixing bowl with hand mixer or whisk.
3. Add almond flour, baking soda, salt and spices. Mix until combined.
4. Chill batter in freezer for 5 - 10 minutes.

5. Scoop chilled batter into 6 large rounds on prepared sheet pan. Press into disk shape with hand.

6. Bake for about 15 minutes, until firm around the edges and golden brown.

7. Remove from oven and let cool about 10 minutes.

8. Serve warm. Or let cool completely and serve room temperature.

raw honey, agave nectar, grade B maple syrup, molasses

Lemon Coconut Bars

Prep Time: 15 minutes

Cook Time: 30 minutes

Servings: 12

INGREDIENTS

Crust

1/2 cup raw cashews

2/3 cup coconut flour

2 cage-free eggs

2 tablespoons coconut oil

2 tablespoons sweetener*

1 tablespoon flaked coconut

1 teaspoon fresh lemon juice

1/2 teaspoon baking soda

1/2 teaspoon vanilla

Filling

2 cage-free eggs

2 cage-free egg yolks

1 cup fresh lemon juice (about 6 lemons)

1/2 cup sweetener*

1/3 - 1/2 cup flaked coconut

2 tablespoons coconut flour

1 teaspoon lemon zest

INSTRUCTIONS

1. Preheat oven to 350 degrees F. Lightly coat rectangular baking dish with coconut oil, or line with parchment.

2. For *Crust*, add cashews and coconut to food processor or bullet blender and process until finely ground. Add remaining *Crust* ingredients to food processor and pulse until dough comes together.

3. Press dough into bottom of baking dish, and slightly up the sides. Dock crust with fork to prevent bubbling.

4. Place crust in oven and bake for 8 - 10 minutes.

5. For *Filling*, beat eggs, egg yolks, lemon juice, lemon zest and sweetener with hand mixer or whisk in medium bowl.

6. Sift in coconut flour and beat to combine. Let mixture sit for 5 minutes. Add flaked coconut and beat again to combine.

7. Pour *Filling* over par baked crust. Place in oven and bake 20 minutes, until center is set but still slightly jiggly.

8. Remove from oven and let cool for 20 minutes. Refrigerate about 20 minutes, until fully set and chilled.

9. Serve chilled or room temperature.

* raw honey or agave nectar

Sweet Potato Cinnamon Rolls

Prep Time: 10 minutes

Cook Time: 20 minutes

Servings: 8

INGREDIENTS

Sweet Potato Roll

1 cup tapioca flour

1/4 - 1/3 cup coconut flour

1 cage-free egg

1/2 cup organic canned yams

1/4 cup warm water

1/4 cup coconut oil

1 - 2 tablespoons sweetener*

1 teaspoon apple cider vinegar

1 teaspoon baking soda

1/2 teaspoon ground cinnamon

1/2 teaspoon nutmeg

1/4 teaspoon ground black pepper

1 teaspoon sea salt

Cinnamon Swirl

4 - 5 dried pitted dates

1 teaspoon tapioca flour

1 tablespoon ground cinnamon

1/4 cup hot water

INSTRUCTIONS

1. Preheat oven to 350 degrees F. Line muffin pan with paper liners or coat with coconut oil. Heat water in small pan over medium heat. Cover cutting board with parchment.

2. For *Cinnamon Swirl*, add dates, tapioca, cinnamon, and hot water to food processor or bullet blender. Process until dates are broken down and thick mixture forms. Set aside.

3. For *Sweet Potato Roll*, sift tapioca flour, 1/4 cup coconut flour, baking soda, salt and spices into In medium bowl.

4. In small bowl, beat egg, yams, sweetener and vinegar with hand mixer or whisk until well combined. Beat in warm water and oil.

5. Add yam mixture to dry ingredients and mix until well combined. If necessary, add coconut flour or water 1 tablespoon at a time to form a soft and slightly sticky dough.

6. Dust parchment covered cutting board and hands with tapioca flour to prevent sticking. Turn dough out onto parchment. Use dusted hands or rolling pin to flatten dough into 1/2 inch thick square.

7. Use spoon or knife to spread *Cinnamon Swirl* evenly over dough. Roll dough into log and cut into 8 slices, approximately 1 - 1 1/2 inch thick.

8. Turn rolls swirl side up and place in prepared muffin pan.

9. Place in oven and bake about 20 minutes, or until edges browned, cinnamon bubbles, and tops are firm.

10. Remove from oven and let cool about 5 minutes.

11. Serve immediately. Or let cool and serve or room temperature or chilled.

*stevia, raw honey or agave nectar

Candied Banana Bread

Prep Time: 5 minutes

Cook Time: 25 minutes

Servings: 9

INGREDIENTS

3/4 cup almond flour

1/2 cup coconut flour

2 cage-free eggs

2 overripe bananas

1/4 sweetener*

2 tablespoons coconut oil

1 tablespoons baking powder

1 tablespoon cinnamon

1 teaspoon vanilla

1/2 teaspoon sea salt

2 firm bananas

4 dried pitted dates

1/4 cup water

INSTRUCTIONS

15. Preheat oven to 350 degrees F. Coat square baking pan with coconut oil or line with parchment.
16. Add pitted dates and water to food processor or bullet blender and process until dates are broken down.

17. Add processed dates to medium pan. Heat pan over medium-high heat.
18. Peel and chop firm bananas. Add to hot dates and sauté until caramelized, about 3 minutes. Remove from heat and set aside.
19. In medium mixing bowl, sift flour, baking powder, cinnamon, vanilla and salt.
20. Beat eggs, overripe bananas, coconut oil and sweetener in separate bowl with hand mixer or whisk. Add to flour mixture and mix to combine. Fold in candied bananas.
21. Pour batter into prepared baking pan and bake for about 25 minutes, or until browned and toothpick inserted into center comes out clean.
22. Let cool at least 5 minutes.
23. Slice and serve warm. Or allow to cool completely and serve room temperature.

NOTE: Bake in oiled loaf pan for about 40 minutes for **Candied Banana Bread** Loaf.

stevia, raw honey or agave nectar

Orange Cranberry Muffins

Prep Time: 5 minutes

Cook Time: 20 minutes

Servings: 12

INGREDIENTS

1 1/2 cups almond flour

2 cage-free eggs

1/2 cup fresh squeezed orange juice (about 2 oranges)

1/4 cup coconut oil

1/4 cup dried cranberries

1 tablespoon orange zest

1 teaspoon baking powder

1/2 teaspoon vanilla

1/2 teaspoon sea salt

INSTRUCTIONS

13. Preheat oven to 350 degrees F. Line muffin pan with paper liners or coconut oil.

14. In medium bowl, beat eggs with hand mixer or whisk until light and a foamy. Add coconut oil, orange juice and zest. Beat well.

15. Sift in almond flour, baking powder, vanilla and salt. Mix until combined. Stir in cranberries.

16. Use ice cream scoop or tablespoon to scoop batter into prepared muffin pan.

17. Bake about 20 minutes, or until toothpick inserted into center comes out clean.

18. Remove from oven and serve warm. Or let cool completely and serve room temperature.

NOTE: Bake in oiled loaf pan for 40 - 45 minutes for **Cranberry Orange Bread**.

stevia, raw honey or agave nectar

Printed in Great Britain
by Amazon

28089263R00066